POETIC MOMENTS
IN TIME

VANESSA WILLIAMS

ISBN-13: 978-0615925141
ISBN-10: 0615925146

Author:
Vanessa Williams

Cover Design by:
The Lyricist Firm

Manufactured in the United States of America

POETIC MOMENTS IN TIME

Vanessa Williams

** AUTHOR'S BIO **

Vanessa Williams was born and raised in Mobile, Alabama. She is an only child of both her parents.

When Vanessa was a child she spent a lot of time playing with toys as any little girl would. In addition to toys she had crayons, paper, and books galore. She loved to paint, color, trace pictures, write and read books. Vanessa was a good student in elementary school and made great grades. When Vanessa was in middle and high school she became a class clown. That was the unofficial start of her comedy career. Everyone was drawn to Vanessa because of her ability to make them laugh. When it came to writing in school Vanessa was the biggest procrastinator. She would wait until the night before to do a writing assignment. The teacher was impressed with the writing ability that Vanessa possessed. Sometimes the projects would be late, and her grades would suffer. She would have achieved an "A"; if she would have been on time, according to her teacher.

As an adult Vanessa developed a love for words and the ability to express them. Poetry became her best friend. It allowed her to get through hard and tough times. Poetry also allowed Vanessa's mind to take a fantastic journey into the land of fantasy. At times of feeling low or high, poetry was the mechanism that got her by.

Vanessa desires to touch others through her poetry. To articulate the feelings of the heart, mind and soul. Diving into the corridors of deep and meaningful thoughts, by embracing the workmanship of freedom of expressions, hoping to leave a lasting poetic impression on you the reader.

** ACKNOWLEDGEMENTS **

I want to thank God, my Lord and Savior for giving me the strength, courage and the ability to write. Without Him I would not be.

I want to thank my beautiful mother Deborah Steele for always supporting and encouraging me and letting me know things will get better.

Thanks for my dad the late Karal Thornton for us getting closer a few years ago.

Thank God for my wonderful and special daughter Andrielle Griffin for her strength and wisdom as a young woman.

Special shout out to my son Joshua Griffin for bringing me joy every time I hear from him.

Thanks for my Grandma Vivian Thornton for always telling me how beautiful I am and how I can do better.

Thanks to my dear Aunt Dorothy for loving my poetry and making me laugh like no other, and for Uncle Prentiss loving me as his favorite niece.

Thanks to my best friend in the whole wide world, Gia Nelson for being there for me in whatever I go through and listening to my poetry over the phone.

Thanks to my cousin Calandra Thomas for keeping it real and being like a sister to me.

Thanks to Alex Lofton aka " Huggy Bear" for allowing me to do my poetry at his open mic.

POETIC MOMENTS IN TIME

Vanessa Williams

Thanks to my Pastor Dr. Derrick E. Houston for being an anointed vessel of God, that ministers to me and keep me grounded in the Word of God.

Thank God for The Lyricist Firm and Co-Founder Mike Sudler aka Poetical Word Play for having such a dynamic vision for us writers to unite by giving birth to our writing careers.

Thanks for your patience, guidance and motivation when some of us were procrastinators.

Thanks for allowing God to use you to help bring out greatness in each of us.

Thanks to all The Firm Family for the collaborations, the support and newfound lifelong friendships.

A special thanks to my entire internet readers for your continued support.

Thanks to all my other family members and friends for your unconditional love and support.

POETIC MOMENTS IN TIME

Vanessa Williams

POETIC MOMENTS IN TIME

Vanessa Williams

*** TABLE OF CONTENTS ***

POETIC MOMENTS IN TIME

Vanessa Williams

POETIC MOMENTS IN TIME

Vanessa Williams

POETIC MOMENTS IN TIME

Vanessa Williams

Vanessa Williams

A CRIPPLED WALK

Why is the pain of everything lingering and not

letting go?

Once you feel relief, something comes along

with another blow.

You have the desire to move ahead, but you

are crippled to move as you feel lead.

Everyone has problems of their own, despite

the good or bad seeds that were sown.

There's a state of emergency within yourself;

To run for freedom and let the past be by itself.

The quest for a better life that's free of drama

and pain.

It's right in your reach if only you could obtain.

Faith is the substance of things hoped for and

the evidence of things not seen.

So walk by it so all of your desires will not be

merely a dream.

Vanessa Williams

A DAY

Driving in the fast lane, trying to keep up the pace. The woes of acceleration of the human race. Detours coming that wasn't a part of the plan. Comptemplating re-arrangements as the traffic stands.

The rat that's in the chase darts without backbone to squeeze through the crack. Poverty stricken memories, never again wanting to go back to lack. Breezes of newness blowing in the wind. Blissful enjoyment with no compromising sin. Traffic jams never sound so good.

Embracing the various voices of the hood. Scan and search the vast majority. Matriculated fraternity and sorority. Soprano, alto, tenor and bass. Chic boutiques with flair and sass. Tongue twirls with the aromas of foods from around the globe.

Allergic reaction around the ear lobe. Smells of gas from the tank. Growling sounds that make stomach sank. Horns honking and a honking. Eyes watching booties that are donking. Anxiety at bay with no med. Dreaming of a sweet reunion of the bed. Centrally parking in whatever zone. Dogs fetching and catching a bone.

Vanessa Williams

A DESIRE TO ACHIEVE

There lies a deep need to achieve.
To believe in yourself and pursue dreams.
One may desire to achieve a higher degree.
To not settle for a mutt, but buy a pedigree.
One may want to achieve a better job.
To achieve happiness and not have to cry or sob.
One may want to achieve a compatible soul mate.
One that's not cheap
but who will take you out on dates.
One may wish to have better blood,
without donated plasma.
One may wish to achieve better health
with no pain or spasms.
One may wish to achieve longer hair
without a wig or a weave.
One may wish to achieve better biceps
and triceps so they can wear short sleeves.
One may wish to achieve
a life free of disease and despair
To not have to worry about receding hair.
One may wish to achieve
breast that doesn't require a bra.
To become the next rising star.
The list can go on and on
about the need to achieve.
All things are possible if we just believe.

Vanessa Williams

A Mid-Life Crisis

The time is flying by so fast. We are often tormented by the thought of how long our life will last. Did we make the best of things placed in our hand? Did we select the right woman or man? Were judgments made right for our kid's sake? After all that we thought we could take. Why does it seem that life is passing us by? No matter how things that upset us make us cry. To pursue a dream after all these years, will it manifest and bring desired cheers? It's hard to stay motivated when your body is screaming in pain. Should you pop a pill or two to distort the brain? When it all wears off, sadly you're the same. Do I give up my dreams and collect a disability check? The horrific thought leaves me a nervous wreck. Am I doing all that I was put on the earth to do? Before God put us on earth, he knew me and you. The crisis that's in the middle of this road, makes me let God carry this load. Shedding hair, fine lines and wrinkles, loose teeth, make you wanna scream good grief! What is happening to me? Trying to have optimism when we have such a slow metabolism. Help I'm at a crossroads in life. I'm standing in the middle and not sure which way to go. Gotta keep smiling despite this race I'm in. Thank God I'm not in it alone. Let us make the best of life before God calls us home.

Vanessa Williams

A PARTY OF ONE

Trying to recover from a past that was shared by two, who would have ever knew, that our hearts would go in separate ways... now I'm walking in a daze… Feeling rather crazed. The urge to break free came... your temper neither I nor you could tame... I will regain my name and leave yours behind. God is healing my heart one day at a time.

Lonely nights with no one there, was something I was already accustomed to... doing everything as if I were already single. I must admit I miss the way you made my body tingle.

The time will come when someone will treat me like a queen, and I will honor him as my king. I wanna be lead on the dance floor. I want to have an opened door. I want to share wine, food and laughs. To massage each other's back. To have no need or lack. Someone to handle my sensual side, someone that's not full of selfishness or pride. To go out to a restaurant and not be asked:

How many is in my party, when it's only a PARTY OF ONE.

Vanessa Williams

A REASON TO WRITE

There are many reasons that may cause me to write. I write when I'm happy and when I'm sad. When I'm joyful, when I'm mad. I write when I'm in a crowd or I write when I'm alone. I write when I'm away or when I'm home. I write when I'm broke and down to my last dollar. I write when stressed and wanna holler. I write when I have problems in my flesh. I write when going thru trials and test. Sometimes I write because it's the safest thing to do. A great alternative to feeling crazed or blue.

Vanessa Williams

A SEASON OF HOPE

This year has flown by and here we are in the midst of holiday celebrations. For those that celebrate Christmas, it is a time of year that we appreciate the birth of our Lord and Savior Jesus Christ. It is a time to share and express love towards our loved ones. For some this time of year brings pain, remorse and depression. Some are lonely and feel that life is not worth living. We must reach out to those that are hurting and offer help, thru encouragement, random acts of kindness and a ear to listen. It's not about material gifts, but it's about the gift of agape love that God provides to us. A love that's unconditional and not judgmental. Let's show the love yall!

Vanessa Williams

A TEAR IN WAITING

There's a tear waiting to fall.
Self-inflicted turmoil having a ball.
Pressing pain exacerbated at the oddest time.
Wishing for a welcomed love of someone being mine.

Mistakes made, ransom paid for.
Secluded realities outlining the shore.
Vast possibilities but none comparing.
Boldness bursting with colors that are daring.
Solitude aggressively winning with an upper hand.
Weakened emotions
that are hard to tolerate or stand.

Harsh elements crippling the quest.
Inquisitive longings to end the test.
Suspended smiles turned upside down.
Relinquished aspirations without a muttered sound.
There's a tear waiting to fall.

Familiar acquaintances of tangible tissue,
sleeve, pillow and all.

Vanessa Williams

ACE OF THE HEART

As the heart wonders to a faraway place

Searching to fill that empty space

Wanting a chance to end this chase

Desiring to finish first place

Trying wholeheartedly to keep up the pace

Blending spices like nutmeg and mace

Trying to perfect the taste

Savoring the tenderness with a baste

Taking time with no haste

Til it's face to face

no failure... but an Ace.

POETIC MOMENTS IN TIME

Vanessa Williams

ALONE JOURNEY

The projector is flashing before my eyes.
The many encountered hellos and good-byes.
Some with many charms,
some with the intent to do harm.
Some with a heart to go the extra mile,
Some not wanting to stay awhile.
Out of all the choices that were made,
Why did I choose the one I did?
May never understand why,
but thank God for two beautiful kids.
New journeys to travel, putting feet to gravel,
walking in territory unknown.
The terrains of changing times,
forsaken past left behind...
direction appearing blown.
Solitude is an antagonist
that does not exemplify the character of me.
In the arms of a leading co-star
is where my heart desires to be.
Dramatically inclined,
without ever trying out for this solo monologue.
Can I please modify the story
to include a second person part?
Rehearsed lines, words intertwined,
starring my " Love"....
to capture my heart.
Journey ahead... sore and worn feet...
persistence no defeat.

Vanessa Williams

AN EMBRACE TO REMEMBER

Your embrace was something to behold.
The strength that came from it,
was stronger than gold.

It gave me hope for a brighter day.
To have a man to love me by not only words to say.

There was power in that hug,
I could have hugged you for days.
Lonely hearts from a distance with desires that blaze.

Can't understand why she can't appreciate
the jewel that you are.
In my book, you're a star.

Working hard week after week.
Determined to provide for your family,
sometimes with no sleep.

Having wisdom beyond your years.
Those that reared you,
deserve some cheers.
Some don't appreciate what they have til it's gone.
Til the loneliness of singlehood
is felt and you're all alone.
As we travel this road of life
with every dream we chase.
Let's never forget that someone could
use an embrace.

Vanessa Williams

ANOTHER BLOW

Thoughts rolling by at the same time. Stopping at the curb of life. Rear view mirror projections of a potential fender bender approaching from afar. Pumping brakes to alert events to slow down and not happen so fast... Before you know it, you're hit with another crash. Insurance in arrears, acceleration of pain and emotional tears. Whiplash effects felt from your head to your neck. Distortion of thoughts, out of alignment due to various subluxations. The pain of life becomes numbing without nerve sensations. Hands reaching and grasping, in a desperation to pull self up and stand again. Staggered gait inflicted with the limps of life. Crippled without crutches, pressing to win, forging ahead at an individual speed. Therapeutic tenacity, courageous calisthenics on a road to restoration with assurance of a full recovery.

Vanessa Williams

ANTICIPATED LOVE

Panoramic views before my eyes.

Beholding the beauty,

interlocking and knitting ties.

Unspoken desires and needs.

lighting fires and planting seeds...

Kind heart overflowing with love,

eager to become whole.

Escaping to freedom and serenity untold.

Vanessa Williams

AWAKEN RAIN

Awaken by the sounds of the gnawing rain.

Deep slumber providing renewal and strength to gain.

Delightful dreams that dance to a melodic tune.

Escalating desires that go thump and boom.

Thunders that roar with all their might.

The lonely wishing

they were in someone's arms tonight.

The sound of the rain on the windowsill.

Provokes thoughts yearning to be revealed.

Drops of rain in the form of tears.

Cleansing sight, erasing fears.

Vanessa Williams

BATTLE WITHIN

Inner turmoil, oozing and spilling. Inner defeats rising and killing. Cut core of torn wounds trying to heal. Persona plastered trying to deal. Deserted paths split down the middle. Rehearsed cognitive riddle. Mind over the matter of facts. Strength on forward and not on back. The atrocities of war bringing pain and sorrow. Wounded souls hoping to see tomorrow. Redemption in reach... Lessons taught and learned. Who wants to teach? Not wanting to get caught in fire that burn... Inner war... Battle within.

BEAT OF LIFE

Cloudy dark days will surely come as you live on earth. Hardship tends embrace some way from birth. Deciding to take on the challenge of life with every blow. Persevering no matter how slow. Keep striving and moving towards your goals, even when things get hot and burn like coals. Laughing at the tears that were shed yesterday. Letting feelings out without being timid on what to say. Making a determination to always progress. Not allowing others to hurt you and cause you to regress. Gallantly walking with your head held high. Exhaling and giving praises with a sigh, of relief that your change has come. Listening to the beat of the drum... as the heart goes on... pumping to a new song...

New adventures and new aspirations. Staying the course without deviations. Graceful spins, turns and dips. Dancing, bowing and thirsty sips. Refreshing expectations of one's self. Musically making the best of life on the treble clef...

Listen! Can you hear the beat? It's getting louder!

The beat of Life.

Vanessa Williams

BIG HEAD WORLD

There once was a girl who had such a big head she didn't know what to do. Constant teasing often made her boo hoo. Different folks would say: oool girl yo head is so big just like yo pappy. They sho know how to make you sad and not happy.

When she was born, they said she had no hair. People would say she was pretty, and then stare. Her mama bought so much grease to smack on her head. God please grow my baby hair, I had enough I declare. Her hair started to grow and soon covered that head. Couldn't wait to straighten with the pressing comb, Ouch mom you burnt me and it's Easter Sunday. Pretty curls, a burnt head soon to be scab, didn't forget the Easter baskets to grab. She always got 2 baskets because she was the only one. Candy, jaxx, toys were all so fun. She has forgotten about going outside to play in the sun. This little girl soon discovered that she couldn't keep her head covered. It was too big for an Easter bonnet. When it didn't fit, she looked and asked who done it. Who shrunk my hat and that's not funny. I'm gonna tell the Easter bunny. That was the beginning of the quest to find a hat to fit her head. Mom they say my head looks like a globe. Girl you better be glad you have hair past your ear lobes. Her high school graduation hat had to be ordered a special size, but that's no surprise. They say big head folks got big brains. Well she's tired of the head jokes and games. As this little girl became an adult, she no longer took insults. So she desired more

POETIC MOMENTS IN TIME

Vanessa Williams

hair to cover the ball. Giving hairdressers a chance by a simple call. Each would say: girl you got a lotta of hair, when they really wanted to say was ur head is big, but they knew if they did, they wouldn't have another gig. She went to a hat shop, with the hope of finding a fancy hat for church. So the owner went on a tedious search. She said I know I will find something to fit your head, she was so happy to be lead to her store. As time passed she said: Damn you do have a big head! She was shocked and said: let me measure your head. It was 23 inches. The woman felt like a pumpkin head. Now she felt mislead, because she couldn't find a hat in her store. This is one place she would not come back to anymore. So she likes to wear different hair and now has a sewn in weave. This story is not hard to believe, because the character is me. Lol!

Vanessa Williams

BLOSSOM FLOWER

Inside of me lies a flower waiting to blossom and bloom. To accentuate the positive minus the gloom. Seeds sown in scattered grounds. Some scattered by the wayside and are never to be found. Plucking away the lifeless petals that doesn't nourish the whole. Living water flowing and nurturing the soul. This flower in neither a perennial or an annual but its constant every day. Pruning for perfection, exposing the beauty in every way. Supportive stem upholding royalty at its finest display. Standing ovation with applause all around. Determined to not welter but always abound. Pressing through the weeds and vines. Gainful experiences over time. Blossom flower to your next phase. Blossom flower despite the craze. Stand tall, firm and with assurance. Allow your power to shine through your endurance.

Vanessa Williams

CAREFREE LOVE

Smell the aroma of flowers blowing in the wind.

Pleasant fragrance permeating from deep within.

Meticulous meadows untouched but kept clean.

Hearts happy with joy,

smiles shine with gleam.

Relaxing and relishing in the presence of our dream.

Appreciating the simple things in life,

such as ice cream.

All doubts and fears all pushed aside.

Humble beginnings not filled with pride.

No hidden agendas, no secret pretenders,

just open and care free.

An old fashioned romance that's meant to be.

POETIC MOMENTS IN TIME

Vanessa Williams

CHERISHING THE MEANING

The holidays are here, the time for much cheer. The desires and satisfactions that come with many things. Makes jolly hearts race and sing. Having a sense of hope for the season. Poetic junctions giving no rhyme or reason. Caroling through the halls from room to room. Forgetting depression and feelings of doom. Cooking delectable delicacies to tantalize the mouth. Recipe competitions with origins from the south. Kissing relatives on their greasy cheeks. Appreciating them as a gift, even the geeks. Romance constantly invading the brain. Slow drops like misty rain. Love giving and receiving, makes many start believing. The presents, no matter the size or worth, cannot be compared to the glorious birth of our Savior and Lord. Let's concretively get on one accord. Lift your hands up in the air.. And wave them like you don't have a care. Praise God for letting you breathe another day. Thank the Lord for the price He had to pay. For the sins of yours and mind. Come on celebrate! It's Christmas time!

POETIC MOMENTS IN TIME

Vanessa Williams

CONTENT

I'm getting more and more content being alone. No

longer needing a man to make me feel I belong.

Getting used to coming and going all by myself.

Really glad to be my own personal chef.

Used to massaging the knots out my butt. Happy be-

ing just me and showing my gut.

It's a joy to shop alone,

without someone asking:

When are we going home?

Joyful eating out at a table for one.

No arguments across the table,

wandering what I done.

Elated to bring in my own bags.

Lifting heavy things, building muscle so I won't have

any sags.

Glad to not have to delete any text.

Proud to be celibate with no sex.

Determined to wait til God says it time. Patiently

waiting for a man that's all mine.

So until then I'm rather content.

POETIC MOMENTS IN TIME

Vanessa Williams

DADDY MAY I

Daddy can I go out to play? Cus daddy I wanna have some fun today? Daddy I'm tired of being in the house. I want a new book daddy, I's tired of reading about a mouse. Daddy can you take me to the library? I wanna be smart like you... Daddy can we stop at the dollar store to buy some super glue. I promise not to put it on my head. I promise Daddy you won't have to send me to bed. Daddy may I have new sandals, and a new dress? I promise daddy I won't make a mess. Daddy can we go to Mickey D'S? I like that food Daddy, it taste better than yours... oops sorry Daddy I didn't mean to say that. Daddy I take that back. Daddy can I have over my friend named Mike? I promise not to let him ride with me at the same time on my bike. Daddy why men have a stick? Daddy the neighbor made me lick. Daddy he told me I was pretty and he gave me some change. Daddy are you ok? Why are you looking strange? Daddy where are you going and why you grabbing your gun? Daddy may I go have some fun? You know I'm your little girl, and daddy you're the best Daddy in the world...

Vanessa Williams

DEEP INSIDE

Deep inside of me is where I wanna go.

Outside forces no longer having a say so.

Who needs feelings and emotions

in these days and time?

People not giving a damn or a dime.

Why has the heart of man become so cold?

Lack of trust, loss of love, many stories to be told.

Everyone pretends they want to be loved

and have it reciprocated.

Why is it so hard to be real and not complicated?

Through hurt, some have vowed to never love again.

Honestly, with this mentality... who wins?

We all have voids that we say we want filled.

The warmth that we once felt is now cold and chilled.

POETIC MOMENTS IN TIME

Vanessa Williams

Perhaps we as humans

don't know what the hell or heavens we want.

Missed opportunities will surely come back to taunt.

Some have become so bitter and strife ridden.

So morality is down,

and carnality is embraced instead of forbidden.

So from this day forward

I won't put up a front or show.

Because *DEEP INSIDE* of me is where I wanna go.

Vanessa Williams

DESIRES OF FIRE

Blooming thoughts

Dispersing all routes

Resistant to tame

Vocal sounds,

designated name

Lingering desires

amidst flames of fire

Tingling sensations

Escalating frustrations

Boisterous with every turn

Muscles contracting with lactic burn

Jumping nerves without a touch

Things longed for and missed so much.

Vanessa Williams

DISCARDED PIECES

The calm of a day

Interrupted by vicious twisted winds

Destruction in seconds

Souls lost with no repentance of sins.

Tornadoes blowing with devastating might.

Darkness boldly making the day appear night.

No time to prepare, no storm shelter to run and hide

The speed of wind nothing to compare... to the sound

that abide.

Loved ones scattered and some never to be found.

Life time possessions that once was held dear

Shattered dreams blackened and deepened with fear

People living life according to the status quo

Had no clue that the winds would blow

Discarded pieces blowing in the wind.

Now...... storm subsided.....

Courage and strength needed.....

to begin again.

Vanessa Williams

DON'T MISTAKE RED ROSES FOR RED FLAGS

Don't mistake red flags for red roses.
No matter how charming he may be or how he poses.
He may claim to have just moved to town. When actually every block he has been around. He may be attentive unlike any other. May claim to be the only one left in his family without a sister or brother. The words he say may flow sweet in your ear. To ease your mind of any apprehension and fear. He may have an accent that you never heard in real life. He says u will be his wife. He starts to ask u to do things u would not normally do. He claims to love and only wanna be with u. Online bank account in your name, claiming to be new to US, needing somewhere to let his money rest. He shut you out of your own account u started for him. Your knight in shining armor is starting to look dim.He promises to shower u with trips and the world. When he has no intentions of making u his girl. When reality hits, u realize he's a counterfeit. When your world starts to crumble down. Your prince charming is nowhere to be found

Vanessa Williams

ENCOURAGING SELF

Yesterday's pain brings lessons learned for to day. Don't stop pursuing your dreams because some road block has come your way. Some setbacks appear big or small. As we continue with life, it's deemed to happen to us all. So if you've been let down by a job that's no longer there. Trust the Lord to direct your path, for your cares He will bear.

Vanessa Williams

FOREVER WITH THEE

Take my hand and guide me through the storm. Allow your arms to shelter me from harm. Forgive me when I act a certain way. Disregard the foolishness I may tend to say. Give me faith when I have constantly been let down. Help me to be joyful despite me wanting to frown. Help me to walk by faith and not not by sight. Give me strength to not give up, but to continually fight. Help me to see myself as you see me. In a royal dress, despite if I feel I look a mess. Help me to focus and be mindful of what I say or do. Grant me happiness when I feel blue. Allow me to love again without any fear. Make me perfect in love Lord, because you are dear. Help me to help those who are in need. Help me to love not only in words but deeds. Restore the years that have been taken away. Reassure me that your love will forever stay. Majestic moments shared between you and me. Father for me to forever reign with thee.

Vanessa Williams

FREE BIRD

I feel like an animal in a cage
Full of hurt, full of rage.
I may be known as Mrs. Glamour
but listen up and hear my clamor.
The armor of my knight is no longer shining.
Please don't think I'm just complaining and whining.
Like Usher said: I'm ready to sign them paper.
Can't wait til my heart starts to taper... off you.
No more dark clouds but an array of blue.
No longer drowning in the sea of my tears, thinking
about the future with doubts and fears.
There will be no longer two,
but I'll be doing me for #1.
No more days of you racking my nerves,
the day is coming for you to be served.
I feel like an animal in a cage. Full of hurt, full of rage.
Waiting for someone to release the latch, not caring
who is in the batch.
Can't wait for others to do for me.
It's in my power to break free.
Yo, this bird wanna fly and sing solo,
so I don't have to worry about ditto.
A bird that's flying high with her own program.
Don't care who's with her or not.
She doesn't give a damn.

Vanessa Williams

FREEDOM WITHIN

The freedom that lies within me I can't explain it.
Freedom to walk, freedom to sing, freedom to answer
a call as it rings
There is a freedom of new beginnings, divorcing the
past behind
There is freedom in wounds that miraculously heal
over time
The freedom to laugh at things that once made you
cry.
The freedom in moving forward and telling past fail-
ures good bye
There is freedom in telling yourself that you can suc-
ceed
There is freedom in helping those that are in need
The freedom that is liberating the very core of my
soul
That freedom is beckoning and commanding me to be
whole
There is freedom in not being a slave to anyone or
yourself
There is freedom in rebuking demons that try to bring
harm or death
The freedom of a fortified place to rest and abide
The freedom in knowing that whatever you go
through, God is at your side

POETIC MOMENTS IN TIME

Vanessa Williams

Freedom cried, freedom smiled, divine strength given
to go an extra mile
Freedom may mean different things for you and me
Freedom is the ability to walk, to move, to see, to be,
to progress, to build, to expand, to forgive........ The
song says: I just got to be free... free.... free........
Thank God for freedom that no man can give or take
away....
Praise Our Lord for the liberty we have today.....
Freedom from guilt and sin......
FREEDOM WITHIN!!!..

Vanessa Williams

FUN IN THE SUN

Sunny skies
Apple pies
Ice cream lick
Ball to kick
Roasting sun
Endless fun
State park
Play til dark
Scab knees
Kid's pleas
Mosquito bites
Flying kites
Sun burn
Waiting til turn
crowded beach
voices screech
Jelly fish
paper dish
Sand castles
no worries or hassles.

Vanessa Williams

GO TELL

Go tell yo pappy that I ain't happy.

Don't mean to put him on blast,

but our love ain't gonna last.

Tell him I's been eyeing these men of coco.

Truth is they a lil' loco.

Hmm I hate to think all of 'em the same.

Their hormones they can't tame.

I's one Sista that loves a good man,

that knows how to treat his girl.

Make her daydream with her hair in a twirl.

Who put a giggle in her belly,

and sweet like apple jelly.

Mmm, a man that don't mind giving a hand,

and taking a stand.

A man that knows how to please and satisfy...

Oool wee!

Can I get a Amen!

Now you go on and tell yo pappy what I said,

cause if he don't tighten up,

someone else will be in his bed.

GOING THROUGH

It's another day in the paradise of my mind. Wishing I was all cleared to start my grind. Tired of feeling like a loser and failure. Tired of seeing visions that end with a blur. My hair is standing on top of my head. It is so difficult to get out of bed. I keep smiling but my eyes are holding back tears. I want to keep thriving and not feel like I've lost years. Does anyone really want a messed up girl like me? Voices keep telling me no, that are the enemy. I must listen to the voice of God because he knows my heart...New start for me.. Tumultuous times reigning in my life. Despite a failed marriage, I still hope to someday be a wife. It's so hard to rise and be on top. I wish that these hard times would just stop. The rent office has no mercy after the third. Fees galore that leave me perturb. No real help down here in the south. I'm blessed to still put food in my mouth. Do I just give up and go sit with those around town that gave up years ago? Painful realities, but with strength I say No! Deliver me God.

Vanessa Williams

GOD'S CHOICE

The strength that lies in me is not of my own.

God's power living in me,

means I'm never alone.

When it seems like I can't take it anymore

God comes along to encourage and restore

I can't explain why I'm the way I am

For I was created by the Great I Am

I appreciate all that God is doing in me

and is continuing to do.

Feels good to hear Him say I CHOOSE YOU!

Vanessa Williams

HARD TIMES

Times are hard everywhere you look around and turn.
Economic disaster has seemed
to hit every home in return.

The cries of single moms are heard by near neighbors.
Trying tenaciously to make ends meet
is worse than labor.

The cry of a child that hasn't enough to eat.
The ridicule he receives at school,
about the shoes on his feet.

The frustration of a man not being able
to hold his own.
Reflections of his past haunt him
in seeds that were sown.

People doing things that they
never imagined they would do.

POETIC MOMENTS IN TIME

Vanessa Williams

Compromising their integrity just to get through.

Families fighting and arguing
with many demeaning shouts.
Resenting having to wait and be called
for a government handout.

Dysfunction on the rise, heavy crime creating demise.
The love of many waxing cold is no surprise.

Bitterness against a society as a whole.
Dreams shattered that were untold.

Opportunity knocking on the doors of some
and not on others.
Distance and defeat separating lovers.

Hard times are everywhere you look around and turn.
Stand strong
and don't allow this economic crisis to burn.

HAVING FEELINGS

Mixed emotions

crying beneath the smile

inner commotions

going the extra mile

Competing without chance

Relentless feelings pushed aside

With time passing with a glance

Revealing truth devoid of pride

Vulnerable without permission

Solitude serving as the norm

Free will without commission

Possibilities every shape and form.

Vanessa Williams

HEART BREAK

Lost hearts searching on new paths. Never again having an opportunity to share baths. Torn memories of what was and what is no more. Longing for unfulfilled dreams, now shattered with no means to restore. Making promises that were not intended to be kept. Tear stained pillows of nights you wept. Reasoning within yourself that this is not what you remember of how love goes... pretending to be resilient but outside it shows... the pain... the rehearsals on the brain... of what was said, what was heard... how the callous ways of humans tend to be absurd. Vowing to never put yourself in the predicament of love again... but deep inside you simply want to conquer and win... At the game of love. Dedicated to all that has ever been heartbroken. Heartbreak hotel is open with many vacancies. Group rate before Valentine's Day is free.

Vanessa Williams

HOLIDAY BLESSINGS

Blessings big and small, allows me to grow and stand tall. No longer living a life of constant defeat. For God's favor has shined on me. He lifted me out of despair and shame, and allowed me to regain my name. The road had bumps, curves and dips. Now new destination and new trips.

Cried tears of depression, now tears of joy. Son grown with a diploma, no longer momma's little boy. Blessed with an humble spirit and peace of mind. God said it's your season to shine. Go be a blessing to others in a managerial way. Don't be too nice this time, but firm at what you say. Lessons were hard and learned, a heart to be my best is what I yearn.

To brighten someone's day with a smile, to offer a special treat by going the extra mile. To visit those who are lonely and hold their hand. To eat and listen to the big bands. Hearing their stories from old. Listening to wisdom to bless my soul. Bingo, bridge & tea time. Scones with zest of lime. Everyone happy and being themselves. Christmas party with staff dressed as elves.

Vanessa Williams

I Don't Know What To Call It

Opened ended questions

Leaving minds thirsting

Relations of the heart

Not impeding the flow

Jugular connection

Systemic drive

Destined to thrive

Concretive and applicable

Efforts applaudable

Bond unthinkable

Pleasing and pleasurable

Riffs and clefs clappable

Feet happy and pattable

Delicious and edible

Non sense deletable

POETIC MOMENTS IN TIME

Vanessa Williams

Sweetness keepable

Teachable and freakable

Lovable and jovial

Reality not unreasonable

So much for that........

Neurons firing sparks on the right and left hemisphere. Make me wanna say oh my dear. Mind drifting to unvisited places. Memory store filled with greedy faces. Circulation flowing at a normal rate. Excuse me Sir, Can I have a date?... ha ha funny! Gotta stay on my grind and make the money. Sock dock and rock it. Don't you dare mock it.... Boom boom boom. Shoo I think it's time to get off the couch and go to my room...

Vanessa Williams

If

If you had been willing to listen to my side,
by pushing away your pride.
Then perhaps things would be differently.
If you had seen that too much was on my plate to
handle and loved without slander.
Not knowing my father's fate,
in a relationship without a date,
constant battles some with and without debate.
A distraction came along and numbed the pain.
Temporary fix to feel loved and sane.
As quick as it came,
it left. Mistakes made,
fallen grace & hard on self.
Help sought to regain ground,
refocused on the Savior I had found. Condemnation
could no longer keep me bound.
Hearing the Lord say He still loves me,
was a beautiful sound.
Changes are sure to come as we live this life.
Whatever life throws you,
don't become bitter with strife. After all we are the
Bride Groom's wife.
If we as humans would learn to admit our faults
without pointing a finger.
Healing could happen & hard feelings would not have
to linger.
If we would learn not to judge & not hold a grudge
then things would be better & not worse!!!

Vanessa Williams

I HEAR RAIN

I can hear the rain beat against my window pane. The sound is soothing to my brain. No need to feel frazzled or insane. The melody is so sweet, reminds me of a special treat. The sound of love in the rain is more desired than a gold chain. The rhythm of rain makes hearts join and sing. The sound of love is in the air, it has style and a compatible flair. The rain is falling and beating on my window pane. My heart is falling and beating for you. Let's listen to the sound of both... let's dance in the rain of love. Love like this only comes from above.

POETIC MOMENTS IN TIME

Vanessa Williams

INWARD JOY

The joy that's inside of me, I can't really explain... It's soothing like a much needed rain... It has taken a while to get to this point... It feels like a high not requiring a joint... Inner wars of the Spirit and flesh... Having victories and giving God my best... Allowing contentment to reign within... Avoiding things to make me compromise and sin... Watching and waiting with great anticipation... Not having to do no process of elimination... The choice of freedom is mine today... Knowing the impossible can happen if I believe and pray... In the midst of trials and many test... God's love has proven to be the very best... After all that's said and done... Joy is one reason God gave his Son.

JOLLY

Tis the season to be jolly! Lots of mischief and lots of folly. First Christmas being alone with no husband or child. No one to drive me wild thru stupidity or passion. No mess to clean up due to inconsiderate trashing. No tense feelings of what I couldn't give or get. Am I missing my kids? U bet. A jolly time for me came when I decided to start fresh. These 7 months has really been a test. At first I was consumed as to whether someone would genuinely love me again. I had developed a complex, no need to pretend. But all along I needed to love me and see my worth. A beautiful only child my mom had given birth. The Lord has been blessing me left and right. I'm no longer bothered by not having a man in my bed at night. A time of celibacy for almost a year. That's big for me my dear. I'm in a state of contentment that only God can give. He give us strength to live. I may not ever walk down the aisle again, and that's fine. Today I have peace of mine. That's better than a carat ring. I'm jolly as can be, doing my thing.

LONGING

Self-fulfillment challenged by a singular me. Words can't describe the way I feel or be. Coming home and no one there. Turn on the teapot with no one to share. Does this supposed to last for the rest of my life? Will I get to say I do again and be someone's wife? So many faces on this internet screen, is there a heart behind the screen just for me? Is my king awaiting and searching and waiting for the same. Is he desiring for an unfound love to take his name? Touch me from a distance and you won't get any resistance. If you and I are meant to be. I don't know who those words belong to, or where they fit. So many avenues that make me say this may be it. Patience is a major key that I must possess. I want God to send the best. Longing hearts, wishing to love and behold. Waiting for the future to unfold. Longing...

Vanessa Williams

LOVE AT BAY

Created moments in time...
Flashes of re-runs in mind
Hands extended and snatched away.
True feelings kept at bay.

Tears streaming down the lacrimal duct.
Questions of why does love have to suck?
Self-pity, not so witty.
I would really prefer to feel giddy.

Swimming to the nearest coast
and realizing erosion had washed it away.
Drifting, floating, lost in the bay...
of turmoil, fear and pain.

Dreams of a place where negativity does not reign.
Sunny forecast expected another day.
Guarding my heart is easy to say.

The song once said:
Don't cry out loud,
learn how to hide your feelings...
But it's not easy to do
when you're a passionate person
that believes in positive dealings.

Operation Heart Mend Again.
Will someday allow me to
experience love that doesn't fail
but win.......

Vanessa Williams

LOVING HIS PRESENCE

The breeze is blowing across my face,
reminding me of God's constant grace.
When I'm feeling low and out of place.
His Spirit gives me strength to pick up the pace.
His favor allows me to take advantage
of what life has to offer.

Making sure I stay in his will,
and not walk as a scoffer.
When life's challenges causes me to feel depleted,
He lets me know with Him,
I'm never defeated.

When things get overwhelming
and I don't have a dime.
He is my provider
and He works things out every single time.

His presence forever reigns in my life.
No longer do I have to be angry and full of strife.
These are some words of encouragement
to those who may be at wits in.

Thank God for a Savior that pardons sin.

LOVING PASSION

Desires of passion seeping through my veins.
Womanhood being expressed in a sensual way.
Loving with all I have til nothing remains.
Illuminating intimacy under the moon,
progressing til the day.

Compassionate caress
as we give each other our very best.
Contentment relaxes me
as I lay and stroke your chest.
Getting familiar with the fragrance
of each of our scents.

Never to be forgotten,
as our minds come together and circumvent.
Understanding the need that each of us possess, al-
lows us to willingly give, with no contest.
Love me like never before,
nothing shameful, nothing to abhor.

I believe in reciprocity because it"s fair and I like to
give expecting all in return. Ignited fire, a heart that
yearns... for you. Secluded away from everyday dis-
tractions. Relishing each other as a coming attraction.
Mmm Caliente Mi amor padre...
twisted tongue not knowing what to say. I love you
papi, you are so hot...

POETIC MOMENTS IN TIME

Vanessa Williams

Love me and don't ever stop...
A storm is brewing in the atmosphere...
Hold me tight my love and take away my fear.
The wind is blowing and thrusting upon the windows
and walls of our chamber. Roars of passion without
passivity echoes in climatic creativity...
loving me deep, loving you strong.... loving each other
all night long...

Vanessa Williams

LOVING THE REAL ME

The night the music played,
it was just for me.
Soulful tunes reminding me I'm free.

Melodies of the heart,
that only time could mend.
Re-acquainting myself with the woman within.

Rediscovering things that I really like.
Envisioning a countryside scene with a mountain bike.

Dancing my way into the arms of a new start.
Never again losing myself and severing my part.

Knowing the real me from the inside out
Embracing my womanhood
with no apprehensions or doubts.

The creative blessings flow from my brain,
let's me know I'm different but not insane.

After all these years I now have the gall,
to say I love myself after all.

POETIC MOMENTS IN TIME

Vanessa Williams

MEOW

Brisky morning, feeling a little frisky. MEOW! Is what the cat said, it was time to get out the bed. A stretch here and there. Hair standing everywhere! Arching the back. No fur ball to hack. Box of litter, no shimmer of glitter. Pouncing from pillar to post, daring eyes and silhouette to boast. After being on a hunt to get something to eat, her demeanor changes from sour to sweet. With belly full and eyes in a blur, she licked herself and let out a purr.

MID LIFE CRISIS

The time is flying by so fast. We are often tormented by the thought of how long our life will last. Did we make the best of things placed in our hand? Did we select the right woman or man?

Were judgments made right for our kid's sake? After all that we thought we could take. Why does it seem that life is passing us by? No matter how things that upset us make us cry. To pursue a dream after all these years, will it manifest and bring desired cheers? It's hard to stay motivated when your body is screaming in pain. Pop a pill or two to distort my brain. When it all wears off, sadly I'm still the same. Do I give up my dreams and collect a disable check? The horrific thought leaves me a nervous wreck. Am I doing all that I was put on the earth to do? Before God put us on earth, he knew me and you. The crisis that's in the middle of this road, makes me let God carry this load. Shedding hair, fine lines and wrinkles, loose teeth, make you wanna scream good grief. What is happening to me. Trying to have optimism when we have such a slow metabolism. Help I'm at a crossroads in life. I'm standing in the middle and not sure which way to go. Gotta keep smiling despite this race I'm in. Thank God I'm not in it alone. Just wanna make the best of life before God calls us home!

Vanessa Williams

MIDNIGHT MADNESS

Heart is guarded against the pain.
Mental madness parading brain.
Power pontificating presentation.
Fierce firings flirtations.
Neurotic neurons dispersing flames.
Matters that are grey and not the same.
Frontal lobes no longer fronting.
Cerebral chaos stopping by without an invite.
Cerebellum moving to the groove of the night.
Skeletal scrimmage throwing a bone to fetch.
Derogatory delusions that are easy to catch.
Filtered frustrations seeping through a sieve.
Rambling gibberish connotations
that connect the dots.
Sugar sweetness that starts to rot.
Smiles with teeth of piano keys
Casting lines in the deepest seas.
Missed elevator that didn't go all the way up.
Flights of steps with water gulps.
Extracting the juices minus the pulp.
Mashed memories with butter salt and pepper.
Fried fantasies with corn balls on the side.
Delicious preparations filled with pride.
Fantastic rehearsals of
the mentally stable.
These are some thoughts
when you no longer have cable.

MIME

Letting the chips fall where they may. Is not always easy to say. Waiting for your change to come, is not always fun. Detaching is not easy, when your heart has been attaching. Captured heart in such a short time...... silent expressions of a mime.......

Vanessa Williams

MIND SPARK

Making an impression on yourself let alone others is a hard thing to do. Inner enemy reminding you of your constant failures, causing you to almost always second guess yourself. Pressing pass feelings of defeat and low esteem. Believing in your heart there is a dream to achieve. Realizing you're not as bad as you think. That you're just as good as the next person. The only difference is that they had the audacity to go for it. Success may be perceived as an illusion of one's worth, reasoned by the back bone of perseverance & positive feeding off the back of others. Concretively expanding the effort with metabolic marathons of, "I can do this." Daring to not let your enemies see you perspire. Proving that you were the right hire. Staying cool & watching your foes become your footstool. Remembering to be wise & not a fool. After long hours, your eyes cross & tiredness set in & you drool. Matriculating by going to school. Staying focused because life's not a walk in the park. It all starts with a mind spark.

MISSING MY FRIEND

You befriended me through my hurt and pain. You showed me you care without being vain. We became close in a very short time. You told me what I needed to hear, though at times it was tart like a lime. I admired you for being so strong. You were mad that you didn't have a butt, but at least your legs were long. The Lord used you to get me back in church. After being a pastor's wife and experiencing hurt. Your church had so much love that was displayed towards me. I knew that this was the way that real Christians were supposed to be. I soon left to go south, with faith spoken out my mouth. We kept in touch despite the miles. Every week we would talk over an hour. One day you called, as always I would answer, you informed me that you were sickened with cancer. My heart fell to the floor, because our friendship was growing more. I prayed for you on a constant basis. Hoping a miracle would happen that would erase this. You pleaded with me to get my own health in check. Metastatic cancer had your life in a wreck. You fought a good fight and though your spirit is absent from the body. You ultimately win, because God through Jesus forgave you of your sin.

I LOVE YOU CHERYL!
I WILL ALWAYS REMEMBER YOU.
THANKS FOR BEING MY FRIEND.

POETIC MOMENTS IN TIME

Vanessa Williams

MIXED EMOTIONS

Sitting alone not knowing whether to laugh or cry. To drive or park. To go in out the dark. Would someone cross my path? So I no longer am a half. I wanna be whole in my body and soul. Why does life hurt so bad? I rather have joy than be sad. I saw a brighter day in my view. But why is there such a strong urge to boo-hoo. I will release the dam and let the tears fall where they may. Hoping tomorrow with be a brighter day. A tear drop on my fingers as I stroke these keys . Would someone give me some tissue please?

Vanessa Williams

MoM

Mom I would like to say... that I love and appreciate you today. Thanks for being there for me in so many ways. You always seem to call at the perfect time. Oftentimes we think of each other at the same time. You were a single parent that raised me your very best. Somehow I still remember as a toddler resting on your chest. You would straighten my hair and give me the prettiest curls. Sometimes that comb would burn me, but Easter was special for your little girl. We have had our ups and downs down through the years. Some words caused hurt and tears. It never took me long to get back on track, because deep down inside I knew you had my back. You have supported me when I didn't have a dime. Every blessing you ever gave was right on time. My desire is to bless you as much as I can. To let you know I'm your number one fan. You are a true southern bell with a heart of gold. You love your lipstick and clothes. I thank the Lord for having a mom like you, for your prayers have got me through. I love you mom and wanted you to know it as well as show it. Keep being the awesome woman that you are. In my book and others book, you are a star.

Vanessa Williams

MOVING AHEAD

Start smiling at life as it passes by.
Stop wasting time on people that make you cry.

Moving ahead emotionally is a must.
As time moves on
someone will be worthy of your trust.

Living in the past only cripples you
to blessings that are ahead.

Free your mind of toxic thoughts and be Spirit lead.
New things and new people are waiting to embrace
you and welcome you in.
Learned lessons will allow you this time to win.

Realize the greatness that God created you to be.
From your sorrow and pain
His son Jesus came to set you free.

Have a determination to be the best in your life.
Devoid of hatred,
bitterness and strife.

Allow love , joy and peace to flow through your heart.
Because one day from this earth we will all depart.

MUSIC MOMENTS

It's easy for me to get caught up in a music moment. It's something that truly sooths my soul. I love all types of music, you name it and if it vibes with me I'm all ears. Songs that bring laughter and some tears. Some allows me to reminiscence through the years. Being an 80's teen hearing classic rock or the Sugar Hill Gang reminds me of how I used to shake my thang. Even though I'm older and still carefree, music still has the same effect on me. Patting my feet, clapping my hands Freedom with every beat, solos or live bands. Imaginations floating on every note and key. All in the comfort of my home without paying a fee. Music provokes feelings of joy, happiness and peace. Music stirs emotions and desires within. Music inspires you to do right or it may tempt you to sin. Music in my ears is like the whispers of a man. Music touches me all over as if a hand. Ah music is so relaxing and it relieves stress. Music motivates you to perform your best. Sipping on a cup of tea... come share a music moment with me.

Vanessa Williams

MY SON, I LOVE YOU

My son, I love you.
I want you to know that my love for you will never
diminish, but will constantly grow.
I was overjoyed when you came into this world.
For your father knew that you were a boy
and not a girl.
You were such a pretty baby boy
with the biggest smile.
Always asking for juice,
that I had hoped would last awhile.
You have always tried to speak for yourself
and represent others.
Even though you and your sister would fight, you
would take up for her like a big brother.
You are coming into your own
and you are an awesome young man.
You have a will and drive, that says: You can.
Never give up on your dreams son,
because God has your heart and hand.
No matter what life throws at you,
always remember...
My Son, I Love You.

Vanessa Williams

NAWL PAUL

A one legged man asked me:
Would you be mine?
Through the dirty clothes and rotten teeth.
I imagined him being good lookin',
somewhere in time.
Didn't wanna dis him in a snap.
Because I have a lot of respect for the handicap.
He had such a sad story
on how he was hit by a car.
Only $20,000 awarded which didn't go very far.
He had 3 sons and 1 was dead.
Felt sorry for the guy,
with so many bad memories in his head.
I don't know if I could be in love,
with a man with only one leg.
So I bought a Sunday paper from him,
so he wouldn't have to beg.
He had the warmest smile on his face.
Apologizing for the teeth he needed to replace.
As I was about to reverse my car,
he moved his wheelchair a little but not far.
He said stay in touch if you can.
I really would like to be your man.
Thinking this guy has some gaul.
I had to tell Paul... Nawl....!!!

NEVER HAD A CHANCE

Never knew that wearing my hood
would mean I was up to no good.
I never knew that walking the streets at night
would cause me much fright.
Never knew the shade of my skin,
was still black in other's eyes.
Had I known my life would have ended that night,
I would have said my good-byes.
I had many dreams and aspirations
like any person with hope.
My demise at the hands of an adult,
leaves my mom in tears & hard to cope.
I've read and heard that others are intimidated
if you're not of their race.
Owning up to one's fears
are difficult for some to face.
I have gone over & over with many riddles,
why did I have to die with only a bag of skittles.
I never had a chance to grow to my fullest potential.
I never had a chance to focus
on the things that are essential...
like how to make an impact
on the world that I was in.
That night only proved how wicked humans
are & full of sin.
I never had a chance to have kids of my own.
Shots fired into my body...
by someone that was grown.
I was a kid with a hood in a hood.

Vanessa Williams

NEW DAY

Awaken from slumber of old. Leaving yesterday behind. New tenacious task to behold. Relishing the sunrise, escaping with the mind. Proclaiming a day of success and not failure. A day of joy not grief. A day of excitement, let me tell ya. A day not burdened but will hold much relief. What does this day have in store for me? I better get dressed so I can see!!!

Vanessa Williams

NIGHT FANTASY

Chasing dreams in the middle of the night.
Laying aside the debris of day without a fight.
Lounging in luxurious fantasies amidst tattered chairs.
Estate with maid and butler with exquisite flairs.

Action packed adventure on the screen.
Rehearsal of things that are not what they seem.
Tapestry of royal blue, purple and brown.
Queen relishing in the glory of her crown.

Passivity no longer around.
Aggressiveness has grown and is standing tall.
Masquerades with formal attire, at grand ball.
Mind drifting into another level of REM.

Where is the king?
Did I forget about him?

Yarning, snoozing,
drifting off to sleep and all the powers that be.
Dreams of a night fantasy.

Vanessa Williams

NOW IS THE TIME

The time has come for me to divorce you... No more apprehensions. But I know what I must do. Detach from your name and reclaim mine. Time to heal wounds over time. Whatever happen with, to have and to hold? Now I'm without and nothing to hold. You promised to love me to the end. My needs you refused to attend. How life has many shifts and turns. Our hearts no longer with love burn. So go along with your life. And seek out for yourself a new wife. I won't hold any grudge for all you did to me or didn't do for me. Christ came to set me free. Little did I know that He would set me free from you. He still has a purpose and a plan minus you being my man. I pray for a chance at love again but if it doesn't happen I still win. My victory is not in staying married to you. But staying married to Christ. The human race that we are in, give us strength to start again. So I say farewell my husband I'm no longer at your side. May God grant you peace and heal your pride. I'm on a serious quest to find me, now is the time you see.

Vanessa Williams

PLANET NESSA

Welcome to Planet Nessa.
Your out of space Contessa.
Land your spaceship on my ground.
Collect your bags in lost and found.
I'm more playful than Venus and Mars.
Take many joyrides with no need for cars.
Hearts evolving around the moon.
Eclipse expected to pass real soon.
Indulge in all I have to offer.
Sunny expectations without a scoffer.
Moon walking on the powder floor.
Appetizing foreplay of what's in store.
Dizzy desires floating in orbit
Only a real spaceman allowed,
that doesn't include Norbit.
Don't go bragging on what you got.
The temperature is moist and hot.
Robotic stick,
Reality flick.
Hypnotic lick,
sexuality click.
Let's end the chase and enjoy my inner and outer
space. It's no disgrace.
Park and ride all night long.
Euphoric melodies of a passionate song.
Welcome to planet Nessa,
feel free to bless her.

Vanessa Williams

PLEASE PILLOW HOLD ME TIGHT

Please pillow hold me tight.
Numb the pain of being alone another night.
Please pillow whisper in my ear.
Take away my anxiety and fear.
Please pillow love me and never let me go.
Please catch my tears as they start to flow.
Pillow please tell me I'm worthy of someone's love.
Please pillow tell me I have beauty like a dove.
Please pillow be with me through thick and thin.
Please pillow sooth me and be a perfect friend.
Please pillow erase every wound.
Please pillow let us harmonize and be in tune.
Please pillow appreciate me for who I am.
Please pillow don't ever put me in a jam.
Please pillow support me in every way.
Please pillow listen to what I say.
Please pillow don't try to run.
Please be sweet to me like a honey bun.
Please pillow lay me down in my bed.
Please pillow let me rest my head.

Vanessa Williams

REALITY HURTS

Reality hurts when you're sitting all alone.
Reality hurts when you have no one to call your own.
Reality hurts when you have no job or means.
Reality hurts when things are not what they seem.
Reality hurts when you're middle-aged.
Reality hurts when life turns a new page.
Reality hurts when you can't make your problems go away.
Reality hurts by the things people say.
Reality hurts when you can't pay your bills.
Reality hurts when you can't make a deal.
Reality hurts when your body is inflicted.
Reality hurts when thoughts are conflicted.
Reality hurts when no one knows who you are.
Reality hurts when an old wound leaves a scar.
Reality hurts when kids don't care like they should.
Reality hurts when you didn't but could.
Reality hurts when someone you love pass.
Reality hurts when you look into a glass.
Reality hurts when no one trust what you say.
Reality hurts when it always appears dark
instead of day.
Reality hurts when you have to
compete just to stay alive.
Reality hurts when it's hard to revive...

POETIC MOMENTS IN TIME

Vanessa Williams

REMEMBERING YOU

It seemed to be a normal day in the USA. People hustling and bustling trying to make ends meet. Corporate meetings being held. Pan handlers on street. Children being kissed at the bus stop. Waiting again to see mom or pop. Surburban commuters crowding the trains. Gridlock alert, make getting to work insane. If only more had called out that day. Not having a clue that their life they would have to ultimately pay. The first tower was struck before many had a break. A disruption with terror with no means to escape. Screams heard from all around. Some not knowing what to do, jumped from stories on high to the ground. As the building started to crumble, the second tower was hit. Thick smoke, burning metal, fire that created a hell on earth pit. The arthosities of war was right here and not somewhere else. History made for centuries on many shelves. Wives losing the love of their life and men losing wives the same. Children without parents, forever scarred in their brain. Remembering the pain. Remembering you.

Vanessa Williams

RESTFUL PLACE

Working hard and not being a slouch. Lounging and being free on my new couch. Moscato in one hand and popcorn in the other, the movie theater kind with extra butter. So many channels don't know what to see. Feel good just being me. New phone don't know the number and never heard the ring. Maybe on my voice mail I will sing. Lots of decorating to do, guess I gotta buy some tools. Hopefully I will know how to use. It will be kinda hard cooking for one when I was used to feeding a house of greedy folks. Appetites that were no joke. I love music much more than TV. Bought some old school jams on CD. Some of them I don't need to hear right now because they on the slow side. Don't need to be thinking about a joy ride. LOL! So I'm just resting in my place.

SEASONS CHANGING

The season is changing. Time for rearranging. Moving things all around. Screeching noises from the sound. Tucking away the old & making room for the new. Delightful mornings sprinkled with dew. Alluring appreciations savored at unexpected times. Charitable contributions given w/ the sounds of bells & chimes. Aromatic fragrances fumigating the air. Fancy attire worn with sophistocated flair. A changing season gives love a special reason. Endearments e pressed with a warm embrace. Peaceful countenance displayed on face. Beholding the beauty of the season. No condemnations, strife or treason. Having pure love for this season...

Vanessa Williams

SECOND TIME AROUND

Cascading flowers

Accolades of festive praise

Attractive adorning attire

Pillars passionately positioned

gleaming smiles of satisfaction

Loved ones from afar and near

Hearts and souls joined as one

Past failures forgotten

Courageous strength starting anew

Giving and receiving gifts of love

Savoring morsels of delicacies

Dancing hand in hand to the tune of love

A foreplay of things to come

Love expressed without any inhibitions

A journey of love intertwined

A vision of me being yours and you being mine.

Vanessa Williams

SEE WHERE IT GOES

Territories unknown
Horizons illuminating above
Welcoming chances not each it's own
Hearts pounding with emotion and love
Realist and dreamer all in one
Giving faith a try without saying I'm done
There's alot that sheer reasoning doesn't comprehend
It's beyond the norm and definitely against the grain
Relinquishing feelings is not an option now or then
Mental battles asking... Are you insane?
One may try and analyze the who's, the what's, the
when's and the how's of the heart
The trajectory will be followed
over the course of time
Connection peculiar and unfeigned from the start
Deep longings that's yours and mine.

Vanessa Williams

SEIZING

A new horizon,

A new day,

A brand new start,

coming your way.

Forget the past,

if it caused you pain,

Cleanse your soul,

with gentle rain.

Embrace new opportunities, that's in store,

Fill your heart,

with joy and love even more.

Vanessa Williams

SELF WAR

Twisted emotions
Hurling down a path unknown
Inner commotions
Railings of remorse of seeds sown
Unintentional afflictions of self-pain
Questions flowing steady like rain
unconventional ways that has no shame
Self-inflicted woes, pity and blame.
Sirens alarming in the center of attention
Secrets held not worth a mention
Catalyst distorting the realm of supportive means
Derogatory dimples that cunningly beam
Kissing an ass that's your own
To appease the failures that were blown
Solitary whispers debating the good and bad
Mental parties to avoid feeling sad
to obliterate. to humiliate. to conjugate to alleviate,
to suffocate the negativity... To lead to productivity...
inner wars attacking the mind must be defeated one
day at a time...

Vanessa Williams

SELF WITHDRAWAL

Misunderstood in a cold world without feelings. Withdrawing self from interactions and dealings. No need to stand up for me, I'm secluded so let me be. Introverted perspectives embracing without remorse. No longer matters about being someone's choice. Turtle tendencies to go within a shell. Memories too painful to confront or tell. Why LOL when stuff ain't funny? Why window shop with no money? Bubbly personality not a requirement to survive. Hustling and bustling, not wanting to have a failure to thrive. stepping back... back... back... into my... Shell..........

SONG OF PRAISE

The blessings of the Lord are in this place...

The blessings of the Lord are in this place...

The blessings of the Lord are in... this place...

are in... this place.

The peace of the Lord is in this place...

The peace of the Lord is in this place...

The peace of the Lord is in this place...

in... this place..

Wherever you are right now... just lift your hands...

Wherever you are right now just lift your hands...

Wherever you are right now just lift your hands.

just lift... your... hands

Praise the Lord... Praise the Lord... Praise the Lord

in... this.... place.

Vanessa Williams

SPRING

Winter being rushed by spring. Beautiful birds rehearsing to sing. Fallen leaves holding a previous life. Trees birthing new ones without strife. Flowers of many colors blossoming anew. Bursting with fragrances with aromas that sooth. Garden preparations to till the land. New lovers walking hand in hand. Heavy wardrobe stored away for next time. Lighter attire welcomed as the sun begins to shine. Refreshing spirit, body and mind. Beholding the beauty without reason or rhyme. Synergy of spring, where every living thing work in harmony.

Vanessa Williams

STILL ALONE OVER THE PHONE

What has the world come to? A place where everyone embraces fantasy than reality. Cyber love affairs all around, loving the chase without the legality. imaginary friends from a picture on a phone. At the end of the day you're still alone. Is this the new way of thinking of how love should be? No hands on, just touching mentally. Copulating from a distance, protected by a condom, called the phone. climatic rings with many tones. Promises of meeting some day in real life. Imaginary proposals of being a wife. No hits from the opposite sex in your everyday world. The intricate web of men on various sites who will be his lucky girl... tonight? Does one want to always have a love that's techno? The heart, the mind, the body says heck no!!! Being spaced out on cyber love seems a bit crazy Like all relationships you can't be lazy. If you want it... do it before the clock tick Before a new search is done with one click. You can meet hundreds and thousands of men and women a day So don't allow your emotions to be played...

Vanessa Williams

STUCK IN THE PAST

Why is it so hard to move forward?
When my mind is stuck in the past?
Investments made that I thought would last.
Can a quarter of a century just be thrown away?
Why didn't you try to convince me to stay?
Your life has moved on quite fine,
but sometimes I wish you were still mine.
How did you manage to move on so quick?
The reality of that blow hurts with every lick.
I know deep down inside you will always miss me.
A continuation of matrimony, my eyes could not see.
The truth is we preached to others
to stay together and work it out.
Us not being able to practice what we preached,
only ended in a shout.
While on this road of singlehood, I see that no one is
perfect but possess some good.
It's about what one is willing to tolerate.
Never forgetting the need to communicate.
The memories will never be forgotten on what I
thought would last.
It's imperative that I move on
and not be stuck in the past.

Vanessa Williams

SWIMMING THROUGH
THE STORM

Swimming towards the ship
that appears to have passed you by.
Under current of emotions with an ocean of tears
with eyes that cry.
Longing to get an upper hand with every stroke.
Deep hidden treasures with guarantees
of never being broke.
The life jacket that seem to expand with age. Doesn't
fit anymore and you're filled
with bitterness and rage.
The overflow of wicked and worldly waves.
Has knocked you down and you're livelihood caves.
Gasping for air as panic invades your lungs.
Distant melodies of songs that you previously sung.
Freestyling your way out of the muck and mire.
Ignited images of yourself
with a will and a passion of fire.
To regain strength needed to persevere and not die.
Inner peace and grace with agility as a butterfly.
Catching up on the years that were lost.
Never again taking a dive, without counting the cost.
Olympic laps of life that tend to kick & squirm.
Malnourishment felt due to sucking worms.
The anticipation of victory is felt
just a few feet ahead.
You're alive & not dead.

Vanessa Williams

THE BEAUTY WITHIN

Doing a self-evaluation is never easy.
Especially when everything,
hasn't always been breezy.
Disappointment after disappointment,
sometimes in one's own self.
Trying to make an impact before your death.
Wasted years spent in a stagnant stage.
Inner conflicts, proliferating rage.
Time passes and you start to grow,
creative confidence projects a radiance that show.
Wisdom exudes,
from the fibrous tissues that connect
every bone and joint.
Mastering the job in being cognitively on point.
Articulating the directions of life,
in the compass of journeying ahead.
Being free and convicted of doing what you feel lead.
Deep in the chambers of the heart,
lies new beginnings and new starts.
Systemically pumping blood to circulate,
as you emancipate yourself,
grasp and take hold...
and love the beauty within!!!

Vanessa Williams

THE BLESSING

The blessings just keep coming my way.
Never losing sight of who gives me another day.
Necessitates my need to pray.
When It seems like all hope is gone,
A major breakthrough comes via the phone.
Putting me back into the leader
He has called me to be.
Letting me know I must walk by sight,
no matter if I can't see.
Past failures tried to keep me from trying again.
The Lord lets me know with Him I can this time win.
My heavenly father is able to meet my every need.
I promise to never again forget to sow a seed.
As I look around,
He is making my life more and more complete
Forging ahead with more strength,
and energy with no depletes.
As the blessings keep coming my way.
I lift my hands and praise my God on this day.

Vanessa Williams

THE DAY I WALKED OUT

The day I walked out was a liberating day for me.
The day I walked out, I knew it was time to be free.
The day I walked out, I had, had enough.
The day I walked out I knew things would be tough.
The day I walked out I only had a few things of my own.
The day I walked out of a marriage that was blown.
The day I walked out emotionally I started to heal.
The day I walked out no more secrets or lies to reveal.
The day I walked out with no money in my pocket.
The day I walked out family sent money like a rocket.
The day I walked out the pain on my son's face... it's hard to erase.
The day I walked out, things that were said to paint me a disgrace.
The day I walked out, I went against the norm.
The day I walked out drenched in mental storms.
The day I walked out, glad I did it while still alive.
The day I walked out, I knew I would survive.
The day I walked out I knew I deserved better if only it came from me.
The day I walked out I was embraced by my dignity.

Vanessa Williams

THE NATURE OF MAN

Challenging times
Changed minds
Disgrace and shame
Derogatory names
Hearts trusted
Agendas busted
Love displayed
Emotions played
Denials heard
Findings absurd
Betrayal lies and deceit
Portrayal of ties with conceit
Cold blustery winds

Blowing and uncovering sin
Severed hands never to write again
Esteem flying from high to low
Lyrical war expressed with every blow
Trying with all means to defame our name
Defensive with no admittance....oh what a shame.
God help us to walk to be more like you.
Help us to love, honor and respect each other because it's
your command.

POETIC MOMENTS IN TIME

Vanessa Williams

Cleanse our heart of hatred, malice and strive.. Convict us to live a righteous life. Allow us to see the real enemy for the deceiver he really is. God I ask this day for hearts to heal. Some may never be friends anymore. Having a clean conscience is something more. Things always happen for a reason. Father God bless us in this season in Jesus name amen!!!

Vanessa Williams

THE POWER
THAT LIES WITHIN

There is power in letting things go
that are not beneficial to the soul,
body or mind.
There is power is leaving a troubled past behind.
There is power in saying no to a previous friend,
that kept you in bondage and sin.
There is power in loving and respecting yourself.
Even when it goes against the norm of everyone else.
There is power in releasing the hold
that seem to paralyze.
There is power in allowing yourself
to blossom before your eyes.
There is power to say yes or no.
There is power behind an opened or closed door.
There is power to rationalize, project, and perceive.
There is power to stigmatize, mislead, or deceive.
There is power to choose happiness or despair.
There is power to tear down or repair.
There is power to be ambiguous or reassured.
There is power to be devious or good.
There is power in a blunder or fall.
There is power in thunder and trees that stand tall.
The power that lies within radiates
and gives life and hope.
The power that lies within
gives us mechanisms to cope.
Thank God for the power of His Spirit,
to keep, guide and protect.

Vanessa Williams

THE TEST

Pulse races as anxiety comes at an all-time high.
Praying God will grant me mercy
and I won't have to sigh.

Microscopic cells that can't to the eye be seen or felt.
Hoping and believing a better hand of cards is dealt.

God has given me many victories through many test.
Lord please don't let it be cancer in my breast.

Allow me to continue to live by your grace.
Righteously before you as I seek your face.

Help me to take better care of the temple I am in.
God give me strength as you embrace me as kin.

Give me a testimony as the intercessors stand proxy.
Let the results be a negative biopsy.

Vanessa Williams

THE WOMAN WITHIN

Looking back over the shoulders of my world. Spoiled only child, lonely little girl. Odd and taken a little strange. A sincere desire for the world to change. Holding my gut in tight, afraid of the terror by night. Expressions of tears without words. Desperate desires to be understood and heard. Wanting to articulate and convey without being mixed up on what to say.

Shyness came and long have gone away. Today I no longer hold my tongue, Like when I was young. Jolly and jovial is the norm for me. Even in solitude I'm happy and free. No longer ashamed to look at my reflection. Able to speak and guard my heart with protection. Life has taught me to love but not be easy.

Radar alert for those that are cheesy. Have learned how to cut ties. Oh by the way I'm known to make mean sweet potato pies. Today I can hold up my chin, because I love the woman within.

Vanessa Williams

THE WOMAN YOU'VE BECOME

The day you were born, you were my special baby girl. You had big eyes and long hair with plenty of curls. You had determination from an early start, and your smile would always melt my heart. You have wisdom far beyond your years. Outspoken person that would cause laughter or tears. At your lowest you never gave up. Never forgetting to ask the Lord to fill your cup. Now an adult with many aspirations, you never gave up despite the frustrations. You graduated with your degree, had all of us filled with glee. Now working on your next degree, because hard times are not what you wanna see. I'm so blessed to have a child like you. You make me happy and cheer me when I'm blue. May God continue to bless you to make a positive impact in the world. I love you my baby girl.

Vanessa Williams

THINKING

Putting up guards
that only you can take down.
Being an object of one's lessons
without a frown.
Self-evaluation
when it's only you taking the test.
Grading system rigged by societal standards
of those deemed the best.
Racing against time
before you ultimately clock out.
Missed punches corrected and submitted proving to
yourself you have clout.
Magnetic strip that gravitates
and draws you in.
Comprehensive package with paper and pen. Writing
stuff that sometimes
don't make any sense.
Captivating imaginations of those
who are mentally dense.
Neuromuscular signals that make you twitch.
I have to end this write right now,
because I'm beginning to itch.

POETIC MOMENTS IN TIME

Vanessa Williams

TIME

Time waits for no man. Many sitting around looking for a hand. Excel and get on your game. Hunger will come to ya if you're lame. Obsessing about what others got. Grab hold and get your share of the pot. No one likes a lazy ass, get up and take a class. No silver spoon in your mouth when you were born. Start being whole and not torn. Time will come and pass, so I command you to get off your ass!

UNBREAKABLE

They're try'na break me, but they can't break what God put back together again. Many may perceive me as a loser, but with the Lord on my side, I conquer and win. They are so ambitious and easy to cut your throat. Having others worried about their next meal and filled with gloat. Deception is a delightful taste on their tongue. Not caring who gets their heads hung. I've learned a long time ago not to put my confidence in man. So no matter what happens to me, my life is in God's hand. God is my provider; He made me a survivor, of the fittest at heart. As I get older, the more wisdom He imparts. So go on world and persecute me, I know my Savior has set me free.

Vanessa Williams

UNEMPLOYMENT

Standing in line to get a grip on life.
Inner wars inner strife...

Worried countenances all around displaying let downs that each has had. Praying that today they will become glad. Hoping this time they would be chosen out the crowd. Going home to family & feeling proud. Expectations heighten as faith fights for a chance. Perhaps the news will rekindle romance. Anger hidden by a smile, to cover how you really feel. Choices made before that day no longer has appeal. To be among the numbers of something that's not great. Vowing if given a chance you will never call out or be late. The mistakes you made while previously making the dollars. Are tormenting lessons that make you scream & holla. Never imagining you're be living with no paycheck, vivid aspirations ending in a wreck. Competing in a market that constantly change. New advances in technology makes the world strange. We must be willing to change with the time, especially if we plan to make another dime. Times are hard, prepare to win, in the world we're in.

Vanessa Williams

WAVES OF TURMOIL

An agonizing cry
coupled with a tumultuous frame of mind
Watered streams released
with a gentle flow of memories left behind
Reasoning rationalized in a formidable way
The taciturnity of emotions
kept at the bay of daring things not to say
The tutelage of defense
relating to the contractions of the heart
Mental wars raging
that's intellectually hard to outwit or outsmart
Ubiquitous fecal matter
flying to the corners of the globe
Many prominent figures asking to be disrobed
The changing of the guards passing
to the next generation
Unresolved issues magnified
with greater proliferation
helpless harnesses worn around the throat
Arrested development stunted choke
Gesticulating in the movement
of life as the wind blow
Some rich,
some destitute without knowing where to go
Gregariously mingling in the gigantic room
of the world
In the end solitude will embrace
every man, woman, boy and girl.

Vanessa Williams

WHISPERS OF WINE

Romantically inclined
with a love as sweet as wine.

Smelling the aromas of cherry,
citrus and wood.
Anticipated wait makes it oh so good.

Tongue swirling around the rim.
Rich bold color like a precious beautiful gem.

Chilled to a temperature that's really cool.
Salivary glands that start to drool.

Taking sips in... nice and slow,
robust flavors tickling with oral sensations.
Relaxation in full gear with no hesitation.

As every swallow is appreciated and taken in.
A warm fuzzy feeling
starts to immediately begin.

Love in its sweetest form,
is able for stress to be transformed.

Whispers of wine is an auditory delight.
Whispers of wine is on the menu tonight.

Vanessa Williams

WINNING ME

The need of self-fulfillment is inherently a part of each of us. Can I achieve this or that is a constant question that one can often ponder upon. Do you believe that you can touch the sky, or is your self-esteem lower than the dirt? Perhaps you were told that you weren't smart, and that you couldn't achieve anything if you tried. Perhaps others believed in you, but you never had the courage to believe in yourself. If you have been given another day to live and breathe, there's still hope for you to soar to a new level. We often spend too much time trying to win the hearts of others and neglect the need to win ourselves. We are all God's creations, unique in our own ways. We are blessed with different talents. We were all put here to be a blessing in some type of way or another to others. Stop being hard on yourself and win you! Pursue your dreams and Praise God for blessing you with you. Love God and you will love yourself.

Vanessa Williams

You Gotta Get Up From Here

Battered abused and misunderstood.
tattered confused and told you were no good.
Searching in the wrong places to numb the pain.
Fighting demons of depression and anxiety,
while on the verge of going insane.
Memories of the wrongdoings of others
play re-runs in your mind.
Electrical shock needed to erase hurt
and leave it behind.
Self-paralysis inflicted upon yourself that prevents
you from forging ahead.
Turmoil dancing with deceit twirling in your head.
As time goes by the inner you starts to gain strength.
Not allowing circumstances to make you bent.
Stripping down to the core of the real you and laying
your garments to the side.
Loving yourself but not being full of pride.
Thinking better of yourself than you did before.
Mental attitude being reprogrammed
and start to restore.
You start to gain the confidence needed to conquer
and win. Holding your head high and lifting your chin.
Being determined to face every fear.
Deciding by telling yourself...
You gotta get up from here.

YOU HAVE A LOT TO SEE

LOST WAGES
BURNING RAGES
INSTINCTS TO HOLLAR
NO CLUE OF THE NEXT DOLLAR
INNER WORTH NOT SEEN
ACCUSATIONS BLOWN TO THE EXTREME
DOING ALL YOU CAN AND STILL NOT ENOUGH
BACK IN THE RACE OF THINGS BEING ROUGH
NEVER GIVEN A WARNING,
ALWAYS TOLD THINGS WERE FINE
BEING LET GO WAS HARD TO PROCESS IN MY MIND
DEMONS OF LOW ESTEEM TRYING TO CORRUPT
DIDN"T KNOW ON THAT DAY
THINGS WOULD BE SO ABRUPT
THE IDEA OF THEM NOT NEEDING ME ANYMORE
JUST WHEN MY INDEPENDENCE
HAD STARTED TO SOAR
THEY NEVER LIKED ME
FROM THE MOMENT I WALKED IN
NEVER HAD A LADY LIKE ME
WITH THE COLOR OF MY SKIN
MAYBE IT'S BECAUSE I NEVER SAID
YES SIR OR YES MAM
IT'S HARD TO SAY I DON'T GIVE A DAMN
INNER URGES TO
WITHDRAW FROM ALL PUBLIC CONTACT
GOD RENEWING MY STRENGTH AND REASSURING HE
HAS MY BACK
I FEEL LIKE TELLING EVERYONE TO JUST LET ME BE

POETIC MOMENTS IN TIME

Vanessa Williams

GOD SAID PUT ON YOUR CLOTHES BECAUSE YOU
HAVE A LOT TO SEE
EVEN IF IT'S ONLY A SMILE ON A CHILD'S FACE
GO AND FEEL THE SUN,
AND BE REMINDED OF MY GRACE
THERE'S GONNA BE TEST AND TRIALS EVERYDAY
STAND STRONG AND DON'T FORGET TO PRAY
THEY NEVER LIKED JESUS WHEN HE WAS AROUND
SO START SMILING BECAUSE YOU HAVE NO REASON
TO BE DOWN
MY GRACE IS SUFFICIENT AND ENOUGH
IT'S WHAT YOU NEED WHEN TIMES ARE TOUGH
YOU STILL HAVE FOOD, A ROOF OVER YOUR HEAD,
EVEN A BED TO REST YOUR HEAD
YOU HAVE A LOT TO SEE..
JUST TRUST ME..
YOU HAVE A LOT TO SEE..

Vanessa Williams

YOU PROMISED

We made a vow that we promised to never break.
You promised to never put our marriage at steak.
You promised to love me til death do us part.
Now I sit in a pool of broken hearts.
You promised to be my best friend.
Now you despise me to no end.
You promised we would never be broke
Now I'm surrounded by bills that choke.
You promised to not let anyone come between us.
Dark secrets, lies and deception kept at a hush.
You promised me that I would be with you for life.
Now you're working on your second wife.
Why it had to be a chick in the church?
who also promised me she would never hurt me
Pastor... Pastor where art thou?
You couldn't even sheppard your kids and wife.
Now we sit scattered fighting demons of strife.
Woe unto them that scatter the sheep!
For you were, the man of the house, but you allowed
the devil to come in.
Strong preachings on deliverance of sin.
Why didn't you stand in the gap for us to stay strong
through every storm. You had her to keep you warm.
You promised to always love me.
Now I promise to love me.